Why Believe in God?

Robert Dawson

Illustrations by
Alice Englander

HUNT &
THORPE

contents

special activities

Activities for you to do are shown by the following symbols:

from the Bible...

Borrow a Bible or get one out of the library, and find out more on the subject in question.

check it out...

Don't just take our word for it – investigate for yourself, and see what you find!

for you to try...

You might need a pen and paper where you see this symbol, or there may be an experiment to do.

talk about it...

If you have some friends or grown-ups with you, talk about how you feel about what you've read.

Introduction

Part 1
Who's in step?
Discover what the majority of the world thinks

Part 2
Look what I found!
Have you wondered where everything comes from?

Part 3
It's obvious (they say)
An argument for God from history

Part 4
The still, small voice
Sometimes God speaks to people personally

Part 5
Nobody's perfect
Why doesn't God stop us from being bad?

Part 6
Move over for me!
God has made you a unique person

Part 7
The disappearing sweet trick
Seeing is not the only way of believing

Part 8
If at first you don't succeed…
People are more than just clever animals

Part 9
Spell books without magic
Lots of evidence of people who believed in God

Part 10
Ow! That hurt!
Why does God let bad things happen?

Part 11
That day Auntie tried to eat the lawn
God uses the ordinary and extraordinary

Part 12
The trial of the century
Look at the evidence and decide for yourself

Introduction

Can you guess what I am holding in my hand right now? Before you answer, think carefully. Whatever it is can't weigh much, or I wouldn't be able to hold it in one hand.

Perhaps you thought of a pen, or pencil. After all, I'm writing this, so that would be a good guess. But that's not what it is in my hand. Here are two clues.

1. I can't see it, and nor could you.
2. You've got it in your hand, too.

Maybe now you guessed air, because it's invisible and it's everywhere. It's not that either. Here's one last clue:

3. It's very, very small. In fact, it isn't even one thing. It's lots. And I've never seen them.

Below: Sometimes, reading about other people's experiences convinces you to believe something.

Did you get it?

The answer's bacteria. There are thousands on my hand all the time – and on yours! Even washing your hands won't get rid of them all.

But how do I know they're there if I can't see them? Well, scientists have seen them through microscopes and told me about them in books. There's no reason why they'd lie to us. I know what they say is right.

There are lots of other things I've never seen that I believe in. Like Henry VIII, for instance. I may not have seen him but I've read about him and even visited his house! So I know there was such a person.

I have never seen you, either. But you must exist, to be reading this. And you must realise that someone, somewhere – me! – must exist to have written this book.

This book is about why many people believe God exists, even though they can't see him, or touch him.

Some people say, "How can there be a God when so many nasty things happen to people?" This book is about why, and how, people keep on believing in God – even when horrible things happen.

And this book is also about why you shouldn't dismiss the idea of God. No-one's saying that you have to believe in him.

But just because you can't see God, or find it difficult to grasp what God is, doesn't mean he doesn't exist.

Above: We know our hands are covered in tiny bacteria – even though we can't see them.

Part 1

Who's in step?

It was passing-out day — the last day's training for the new soldiers before they went off to join their units. Early in the morning, they polished their buttons until they shone, dubbed their boots until you could have seen your face in the toe caps, and ironed sharp, neat creases into their uniforms.

"You all look very smart," said the Sergeant Major. "Your families will be proud of you!"

Shortly before 2 o'clock, they stood to attention on the drill square. If the soldiers had been allowed to look up, they would have seen their families seated around the square – mums and dads, sisters and brothers, aunts and uncles, grannies and grandads. Each onlooker was gazing down with pride at their own smart relative.

The weeks of tough training and hard discipline had paid off. This was their special day, the passing-out parade, and every man and woman in the squad was proud of what they had achieved.

"Leeeeeeft turn!" the Sergeant Major barked. The whole parade turned. It didn't matter that some were tall and some short, some men, some women, some overweight, some pencil-thin. They moved as one.

"By the right! Quiiiiiiick march!"

The whole parade set off. Every click of their feet was in time, except one. Thirty-nine of the forty right arms moved up and down exactly as one. All but one left leg moved in perfect harmony.

The onlookers weren't sure what to do. Slowly, the clapping petered out. The cheering became a murmur of questioning voices.

"Hey, look at that!"

"What on Earth's going on?"

Thirty-nine of the forty soldiers were marching together, but one was obviously out of step. When his left leg should have gone

why believe in God?   5

forward, it was his right; the swing of his arms was the opposite of what it should be.

The Sergeant Major looked as if he was going to burst a blood vessel. Up on the rostrum, the General was clearly not happy. The senior officers around him either scowled or looked worried.

The crowd grew quiet. Suddenly, there was a loud woman's voice: "Eee, look at that! Our Johnny's the only one in step!"

Who's right?

Johnny's mum was so sure her son was right she thought that everyone else must be mistaken. What do you think?

Worldwide, far more people believe in God than don't. In many countries, virtually every person believes in the existence of God. They haven't any doubt. Someone who doesn't is the exception. So who's right, who's wrong? Is it likely that nearly everyone in the world is wrong, and that all those people are the ones out of step?

What's your opinion?

Below: If most people believe in one thing, and just a few in another, who's right?

check it out...

PEOPLE OF THE WORLD AND THEIR BELIEFS

The majority of people belong to one or other of five main religions. They are Christianity, Islam, Judaism, Buddhism and Hinduism. Each religion has split into different groups, though their main beliefs remain the same. For instance, Christianity includes Catholics, Protestants and Orthodox believers; Islam has Shi-ites and Sufis, and Buddhism, Amida and Zen.

Smaller religions also exist, like Jainism (an early Indian religion), Confucianism (originally a Chinese religion), Taoism, found mainly in China, and Zoroastrianism (originally a Persian religion, now found almost entirely in India.) Some people – humanists, for instance – have no religious beliefs.

why believe in God?

Part 2

Look what I found!

Do you remember the story of Robinson Crusoe? He thought he was the only person on the island where he'd been shipwrecked, until one day he found a footprint in the sand.

Left: You have to decide where the watch came from.

Imagine you lived on an island and were sure you were its only inhabitant. Then one day, you're just strolling along a path – that *you* made – and you find a cheap wrist watch.

You are absolutely certain that it wasn't there ever before.

What do you think? If there isn't someone there to discuss it with, think it through in your mind and decide.

The answer would be any one of the possibilities. Of course, it could be that a bird such as a magpie or jackdaw found the watch on another island and just happened to drop it on your path.

But one thing is for sure. The watch didn't really appear out of nowhere. Before it appeared, someone owned it, before that someone made it and before that, someone designed it.

Some people who believe in God say that the whole of the

talk about it...

Whose watch is it?

1. Someone who dropped it?

2. The person who designed it?

3. The person who made it?

4. Someone who put it there deliberately for you to find?

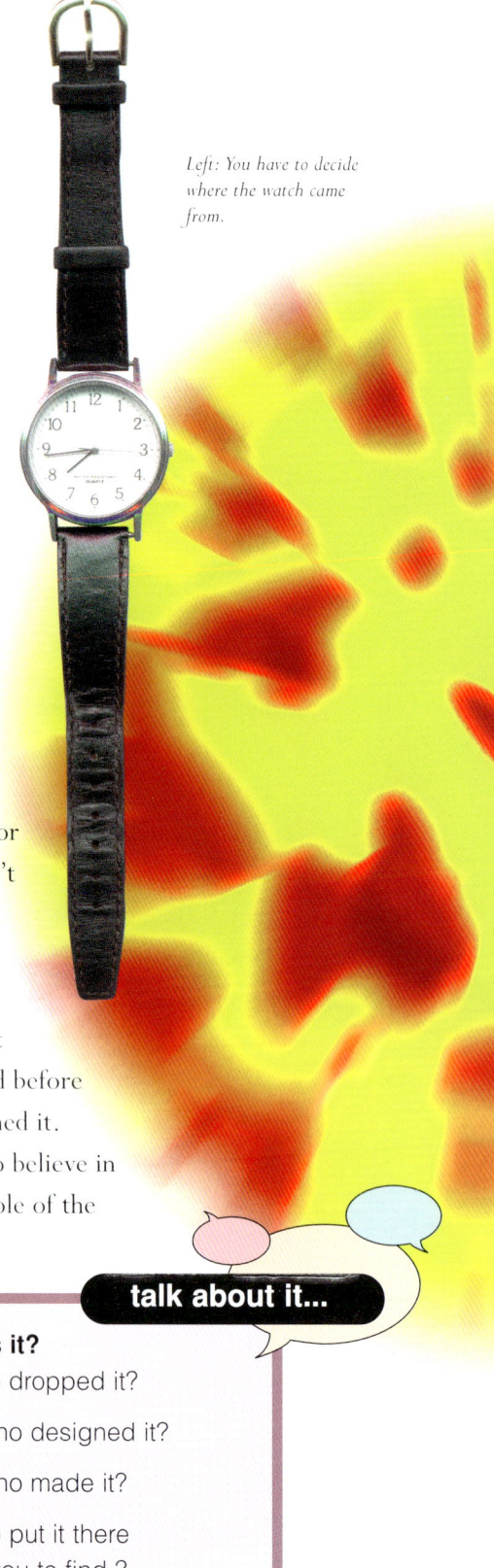

why believe in God? 7

Above: Thomas Aquinas surprised everyone when he observed that the stars moved.

Below: Some people think the Universe was entirely the creation of God.

Above: Many scientists believe in the 'Big Bang' – a massive explosion that created the Universe.

Universe, including our planet, is like that watch. Just by existing, the design (or Universe) proves that something (God) designed it. Others think that the design has been put there deliberately to prove to us that there must be a God who made it.

Over 700 years ago, Thomas Aquinas, an Italian monk, noticed that stars were not still in the sky, but moved. Therefore, he said, there must a supreme force that makes this happen.

Today some scientists say that the Universe wasn't 'designed' at all. They say that it grew out of a series of chance chemical and atomic reactions. They say that there was some kind of huge cosmological explosion which created everything – the 'Big Bang'.

To which religious people would ask, why did the explosion happen? Where did the things which became the Universe come from in the first place? Is it really possible that something so complex happened by chance? In other words, could the watch have made itself?

It doesn't have to follow that whoever designs something also made it. We know that machines can make things (such as watches). But the machines can't make things by themselves. They need us to provide them with the design for the watch.

If there hadn't been a designer, there couldn't have been a watch.

And if there hadn't been a designer, there couldn't have been a universe.

So there must be a God.

why believe in God?

Part 3

It's obvious (they say)

About 200 years before Thomas Aquinas, another Italian monk came up with his own way of looking at how we know that God exists.

Below: You can imagine an ideal situation — but that doesn't mean it exists!

talk about it...

Think of the biggest thing you can possibly imagine...

GOD?

...now think of the most intelligent...

GOD?

...and now the most powerful.

GOD?

Anselm was abbot of Bec, a monastery in Normandy. Some years after William the Conqueror invaded and conquered England in 1066, the King searched round for a new Archbishop of Canterbury. He picked Anselm, who took over at Canterbury in 1093. People kept asking Anselm how he could prove that God existed.

Anselm thought about the question. He gave a complicated answer. He said nobody could think of anything greater than God. But to think of God, you have to have the idea. The idea couldn't just have come into your head on its own. Because if it had, it would be one of your ideas and not the greatest thing you could think of. If it was only your idea, it wouldn't exist anywhere else. So the idea must exist, because not only you have it. Therefore God exists.

Think of it another way. Read these two sentences:

Some black dogs bark.

Some black dogs exist.

The first of these must be true, but the second is nonsense! If the dog is black, it must be there!

A philosopher once suggested that everything that existed only did so in his mind. In other words, you and I aren't really here, unless he's thinking of us (which, the argument goes, he must be at the moment!) That's a very similar argument to Anselm's. And I don't believe it, any more than you do!

However, some people say that to dismiss Anselm is wrong. He wasn't trying to prove the existence of God only with his argument. There was much more to it.

It was something to add to the other reasons we have for believing in God.

We don't only have to have faith that God exists, what happens to us proves God is there. Anselm's argument is simply another way of looking at the same thing.

Below: Ideas about God build, one on another, like links in a chain.

Anselm's description has been called a conjuring trick by some people. For instance, I can think of the most perfect holiday beach. On it, there's everything I want: the sea is perfect, splashing when I want it to, lapping my toes when they need cooling, keeping away when they don't. The sand is golden, the sea blue, the sun warm (but not too hot), there's a never-ending supply of ice creams and cold drinks (free, of course), no wasps or flies, and no other people except those I like.

But just because I can think of it, doesn't mean that such a perfect beach really exists.

Part 4

The still, small voice

Some people believe that when they stop and listen, sometimes God speaks to them. The still, small voice of God is mentioned several times in the Bible (try reading 1 KINGS 19:12).

Left: To hear God's voice you must be ready to listen.

Right: There are many examples of God's message being given in a vision or a dream.

check it out...

Listen. What can you hear? Just close your eyes and sit quietly for a few moments. Then open them again and make a list of all the noises you heard.
If others have done this, too, see if you heard the same things.

When I was nine, I heard the voice for myself.

I'd been to Sunday School and the teacher had said that money was needed for the church's building repairs.

I had a few weeks of pocket money saved up and now I knew what I wanted to do with it. Without letting anyone see, I put it into the collection box on my way out of church.

That night, just as I was falling asleep, I suddenly heard someone calling my name. I sat up in bed. My room was bathed in a strange golden light. I didn't feel afraid, just very happy.

Someone was speaking to me, but I couldn't see anyone. This Someone told me I had done well. I believe it was God, or else a messenger from God. One or two other religious things had happened to me before and I have had several since. So have lots of other people.

Ordinary people from all over the world have had experiences where they believe God

why believe in God?

Above: The Bible is full of accounts of people who heard God.

Above right: The night of Jesus's birth, shepherds were visited by God's messenger, who gave them the news.

has spoken to them, or done something for them, which only God could do. In the *Bible* many people saw visions or experienced dreams sent by God. But not every vision or dream comes from God. A dream may be just a wish fulfilment. Many dreams have no religious meanings.

You don't have to hear God actually speaking. God can and does speak to us in a variety of ways. Christians believe that God's 'voice' may be most clearly heard as they read the *Bible*. God also speaks to us through our consciences. Consciences which are educated in God's ways tell us the difference between right and wrong. You may feel a certainty about a course of action that God wishes you to do something. Or you may get a sign that God wants something to happen or has made something happen. But when God wants you for something, you will know.

Can all those people who think God has given them a message be wrong? Or is there actually a God?

Just listen for that still, small voice. One day if you haven't already, you might find out for yourself.

But check it out. God will never ask you to do something that is wrong.

Part 5

Nobody's perfect

Little Jack Horner sat in a corner, eating his Christmas pie. He put in his thumb and pulled out a plum, And said, "What a good boy am I!" His mum probably thought very differently. Sticking a finger into someone's pie ruins the pie. But then, nobody's perfect.

Here's a real-life example. In a school, a teacher was telling a girl off who'd stolen an old lady's wheelchair and wrecked it. The girl explained that her friend 'told' her to do it. The teacher asked the girl if she always did what she was told.

"Of course!"

"So, if I tell you to bang your head on that door, you'll do it?"

Without another word, the girl went to the door, banged her head on it – and knocked herself out!

So who was in the wrong?

talk about it...

Think about it. If there's a group of you, talk about it together. It's not a simple answer, as you'll probably have found.

The teacher told her to hit her own head, but not to knock herself out.

Perhaps the girl was being a bit too smart, or maybe she really did think she should do as she was told.

You may think that only someone who took and wrecked a pensioner's wheelchair would be silly enough to do that. You never would.

But surely you've done other things you shouldn't. After all, nobody's perfect!

why believe in God?

from the Bible...

In the Bible, there's a bit which actually says this:

When I was a child, I talked like a child, I thought like a child, I reasoned like a child. When I became a man, I put childish ways behind me.

1 Corinthians 13:11-12

New International Version translation

Left: The difference between right and wrong has to be explained.

Below: God knows everything. So why doesn't he stop bad things from happening?

Think of something you've done wrong. If you're with a group, you don't need to say what it was out loud unless you really want to. But why didn't your mum or dad or someone else stop you? Maybe they weren't near at the time, or maybe you did it without telling anyone?

If God is everywhere and knows everything – which is what holy books and religious leaders tell us – God must know when we do something we shouldn't.

So why doesn't he stop us? Is it because God's too busy? Or doesn't really care? Perhaps there isn't a God anyway to do something about it?

Let's go back to the incident with the girl who wrecked the wheelchair. Even if the teacher was to blame for the girl knocking herself out, the teacher had nothing to do with the theft of the wheelchair.

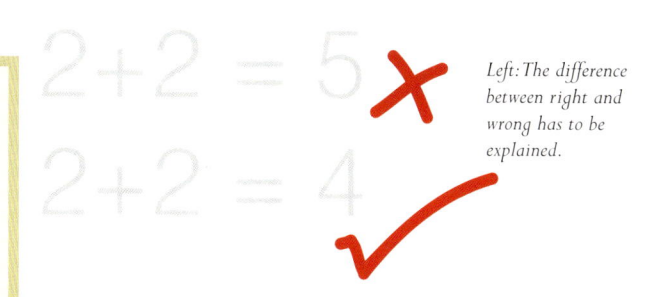

There's something else about teachers. Why do we need them? The fact is, they tell us how to do things that we couldn't do before. Without someone to tell us how, there are lots of things we wouldn't be able to do.

You understand a lot more now than you did when you were a very young child. We have to learn as we go along.

The way we learn is to make mistakes and avoid those mistakes next time. Just like in Maths. Your maths teacher is there to let you know when you've got a sum wrong and explain how to do it right.

Which is like God. God wants us to learn about things to do with God, and with the spirit or soul. He wants us to become better people as we grow older. When we make a mistake, many people think God shows us, one way or another, where we went wrong.

When bad things happen, they're not meant by God, any more than your mum and dad want you to steal a wheelchair, or your maths teacher wants you to get a sum wrong. But the important thing they all want is for you to learn from your mistake and become a better person. Which is just like God.

And if that's so, there must be God.

Part 6

Move over for me!

Above: Even identical twins are different.

Who's the most important person in your life? I'll bet you said your mum or dad, your best friend, or a brother or sister.

These are **all** Very Important People without whom life would be pretty grotty. Imagine, if you had no family or friends. There would be no-one for you to talk to about the things which really matter to you.

Without them, you wouldn't amount to much. Most people would agree that other people are very important to them.

Now try the question again, but this time, be very selfish.

Yes, *you* are the most important person in your life! That may sound a selfish answer, but it's true. You can't live without you. Or breathe, eat or drink or anything else.

And there's something else very special about you: you're unique! Out of all the millions upon millions of people in the world, there's no-one else exactly like you.

It's possible there's someone who looks the spitting image of you - a twin, or someone who just happens to look very like you. But there is no-one identical to you.

Above: Your fingerprint is the only one of the unique things about you.

why believe in God?   15

Only you have exactly your personality, only one DNA strip exactly matches you.

Even your fingerprints aren't possessed by anyone else. That's an incredible thought! If you were an old postage stamp, you'd be worth millions! (Maybe your family or friends think you are, anyway!)

Because we are all unique (though of course we are very similar to each other in some ways, too), we grow up in different ways. The things which happen to us from the moment we are born make us different, too, because of the way we discover and react to the world around us. Every single thing that happens to us in life makes us a little bit more different. Which helps explain why your Great Aunt Rene (or whoever) is a scowling old grump while her sister is a poppet!

So the way we're made (our DNA), and what's happened to us so far, are going to affect the way we think about things. Which includes how we feel when it comes to believing in God. You might have had lots of things happen in life which make you believe in God, or things which have made you very doubtful and unwilling to believe.

Some children who have grown up with a violent, cruel and abusive father, may find it very difficult to picture God as a loving heavenly Father.

Seeking God is a bit like climbing a mountain that has lots of different paths up to the top. Just because you might choose one route, and someone else goes a different way, it doesn't mean you're climbing different mountains or that it'll be different at the top.

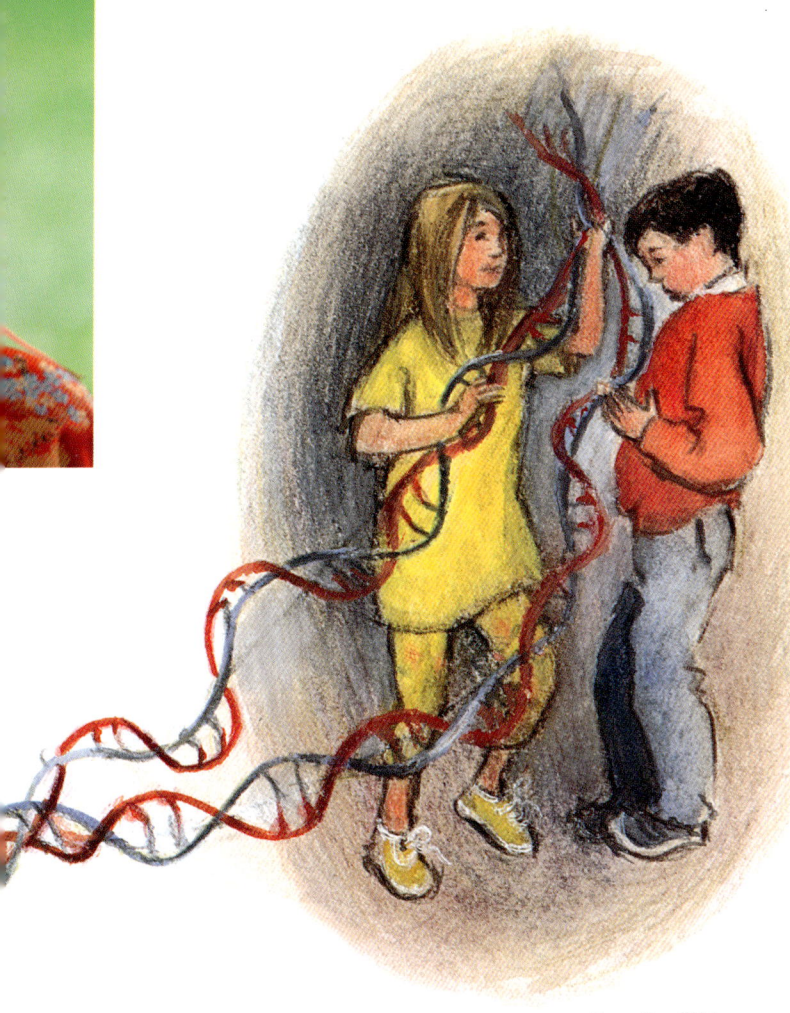

Above: Your DNA might be similar to your brother's or sister's – but it won't be identitcal.

for you to try...

Now a task. Look up in other books about deoxyribonucleic acid (DNA) You can draw an example of a DNA strip if you wish. Especially, try and find in what ways the DNA plan differs from one person to another, and which bits are common to most or even all people.

Part 7

The disappearing sweet trick

We may all be unique, but in some ways we're all the same. Find out for yourself! Here are a couple of things you can try out on a young brother or sister, or someone else's (if you can borrow one!). My favourite involves a sweet. If the baby's no more than eighteen months, you can make them believe you're an amazing magician!

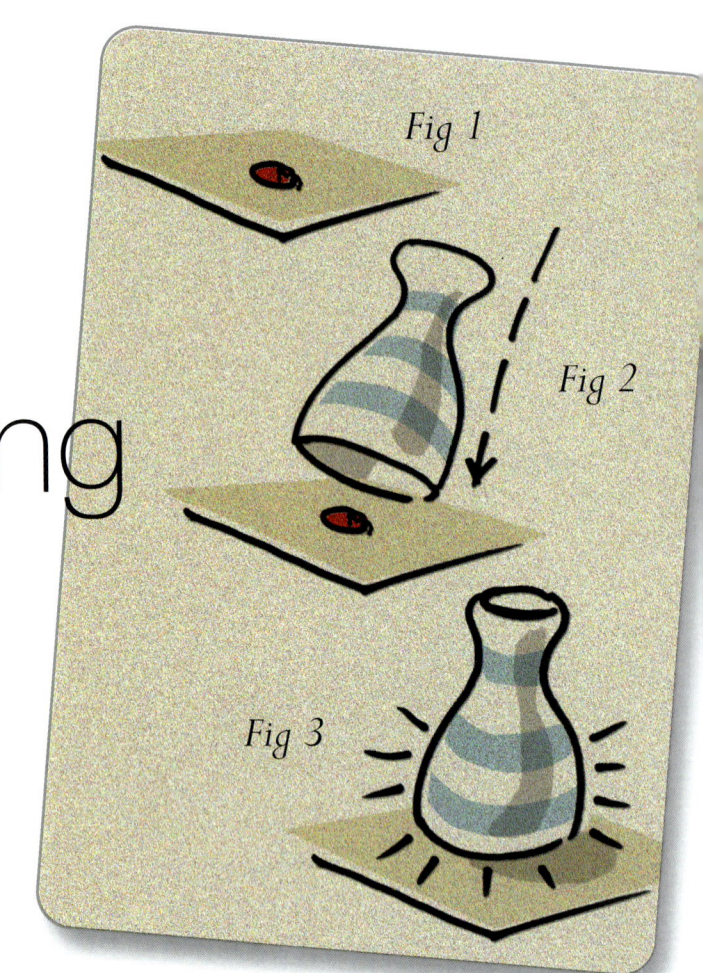

Fig 1

Fig 2

Fig 3

for you to try...

Find an egg cup or plastic beaker and a sweet. Check with an adult that the sweet is OK for the baby to eat and won't choke them. A jelly tot is ideal. Sit opposite the youngster. Show them the sweet, then, as they watch you do it, put it under the upturned egg cup or beaker.

If they haven't reached a certain point of learning yet, they'll think the sweet's disappeared off the face of the Earth! Honest! Because they can't see it, they'll think it's no longer there! They might look round but it'll never occur to them that it's under the cup! That doesn't mean they're thick. They just haven't learned yet that because something is no longer visible, it doesn't necessarily mean it's gone forever.

Show them the sweet under the cup. As they watch, put the cup over again.
They'll still think it's gone!

why believe in God?

Left: If a baby can't see a sweet, he or she will think it isn't there.

Right: The same amount of liquid in different beakers can look very different.

At a certain age, a young child learns that the sweet's still there. If your 'victim' isn't fooled, try this experiment. Get a small plastic jug of orange juice or water. Take two empty plastic beakers – one should be tall and thin and the other, short and fat. Pour the orange into the tall thin beaker, then pour the same liquid into the short fat.

It's obvious to you that there's the same amount of liquid whichever container it's in. But ask the youngster which container had most drink. They'll pick one or the other, thinking that from the shape, one has more.

So what's all this got to do with God?

Simply this: when you were younger, you'd have been fooled by these tricks, too.

When you were tiny, you'd have thought that the sweet had gone for ever, even though you'd just seen it go under the beaker.

And when you were a little older, you'd have thought there was more drink in one container than the other (you could have gone for either).

You believed only the evidence of your own eyes. The sweet had gone, it no longer existed. The drink in the tall thin beaker had more because the drink went higher (or, with the short fat one, spread out more).

Which is exactly like God. We can't see God therefore God can't be there. Even though someone else knows exactly where God is (like with the sweet), we don't believe it because it's not possible.

But just because we can't see God, or think God works in a particular way, doesn't mean God isn't there. There's lots of other things we can't see either, but it doesn't mean they don't exist.

Does it?

Below: Just because you can't see the wind, that doesn't mean it's not there.

Part 8

If at first you don't succeed

A fantastic view, a wonderful picture, a piece of jewellery, a pretty face…we all like to look at beautiful things. It's one of the things which makes us human. It would be difficult to imagine a dog standing on a cliff top and saying to itself, "What a stunning view this is!"

Which isn't to suggest that the dog might not be enjoying the smells, or the sheer freedom of being off its lead.

We are similar to other mammals, but we have an extra, 'something' that they don't. Some people would say it was a mind or soul or spirit. Through this, we have capacities for thought and actions which ordinary mammals don't have.

For the moment, let's assume that there's no God. Some scientists make that claim, saying that we have developed (or evolved) and are simply a kind of advanced animal.

But if that's true, why are we so different from other creatures? Why do we understand things in a different way?

For instance – and don't try this for real – imagine you snatch a bone off a strange dog. What's likely to happen?

Above: No dog is happy to part with a bone.

Left: Only a human would climb a mountain purely to enjoy the view.

why believe in God?

talk about it...

1. The dog will think, "Splendid! So-and-so wants my bone. Their need is greater than mine. They're welcome!"

2. The dog will growl, snap or bite.

3. The dog will snatch the bone back and if your hand's in the way…

Which of the three is most likely?

It's hard to imagine any dog willingly parting with the bone. If it does, it won't be because the animal cares more about you than itself. The dog will only give up the bone if it is afraid of you, or if it thinks you are more powerful. Because that's the way dogs think. On the other hand, it's quite possible that you'd give your last piece of chocolate to the dog. Or even to a brother or sister! Because you like them and care about them.

The spiritual ladder

Just as our body grows, our spirit grows and we progress from one step to another of what experts call the spiritual ladder.

Most people agree these are the 'rungs' of the things we should do to get on each level:

1. Doing things only so as not to be punished.
2. Doing things mainly because you want to do them.
3. Doing things so that others are pleased with you.
4. Doing things because they seem like the right things to do.
5. Doing things so we don't upset other people.
6. Doing things because they are for the benefit of all people, but not necessarily ourselves.

It's very unlikely you're on the sixth (top) level yet, but one day you might be. Many dogs, on the other hand, never get off the first level. Guide dogs are an exception to this.

So we all have this special 'extra' spiritual way in us which normal animals don't.

Here's a question. If those who say we developed only as a kind of animal are right, why do we have this difference? Where has it come from? This isn't simply a question of whether we're more or less intelligent.

If we are only descendants of animals, why have we become so different?

And those who believe in God would answer, "Because there is a God, who has a special purpose for us."

Right: You can help other people on the spiritual ladder, as well as climbing it yourself.

why believe in God?

Part 9

Spell books without magic

Every religion in the world has some kind of holy book. In each one you'll find instructions from God or his messengers, prayers, and stories about the experiences of human beings in their dealings with God.

check it out...

In books, read accounts of Moses receiving the Ten Commandments, Mohammed reciting the *Koran*, and the letters of St. Paul. Notice that several suffered because of their experience.

The Bible; *Exodus 19: 20 - 25 and 20: 1 - 22*;
The Koran; *Ch. 87 (The Most High)*; general book on Islam and its founding;
The Bible; *1 Corinthians 1:1*; *Galatians 1: 1-2*.

Every religious book is made up in this kind of way. Some people believe that holy books were personally written under the direct influence of God.

For instance, in the Christian *Old Testament* and the Jewish *Talmud*, five books (known as the *Pentateuch*) were said to have been written by Moses. The *Koran*, the holy book of the Muslims, claims to have been written by the Prophet Mohammed under the guidance of an angel. Joseph Smith, who wrote the holy book for the Church of the Latter Day Saints (the Mormons) also claimed angelic guidance.

The Christian *New Testament* contains several letters written by St. Paul. Jesus Christ said he himself was God's 'Word'. His words were written down by the first of his followers.

Right: Some holy books are said to have been written at the direction of God.

why believe in God? 21

Right: In the Bible, God sometimes uses nature to punish people.

for you to try...

Imagine you are one of the people who wrote the holy scriptures. From one of the holy books, find the story of Abraham – Christian, Jewish and Islamic writings all have it: The Koran; *Chapter 14*, The Bible; *Genesis 12 - 18*; The Talmud; *same reference*.

Read the story to yourself, or to the rest of your group, if you're in one. Then write down the story.

Now compare your version with the original. Although the basic story is the same, many of the words and phrases you used will be different from the original. How does this help to explain why versions in holy books differ slightly?

Some people dismiss holy books because of such differences. They say they're not consistent. In some places, for instance, God is shown as a loving God who cares about us all. Elsewhere, God seems to be punishing us for the things we've done wrong.

Here's a question

Why does your teacher sometimes get cross with someone in class? Is it because they don't like that child, or because they want the child to do better?

The answer's pretty obvious, and that helps to explain why God might not always seem to be loving and caring. In any case, as you've read, holy books are partly about the experiences people have had with God.

Which means, it's what people *think* their experience is. If God seems to destroy a city, it might actually have nothing to do with God at all. But the people who witnessed it think it is was God punishing them, because they've done something wrong.

According to Genesis 19:12-29, God said that he would destroy the cities of Sodom and Gomorrah because their people were so wicked. Lot warned his sons-in-law to flee from Sodom with him and his wife and two daughters. But they thought he was joking and so were killed because they ignored the warning.

Of course, if there isn't God, it would explain why such things happen. But it wouldn't explain why some people know to escape, and why the writers of holy books are so consistent in the things they write.

The writers could be wrong. Those who read the books and believe could be wrong too.

But as we saw in Part 1, that's an awful lot of people who would have to be wrong!

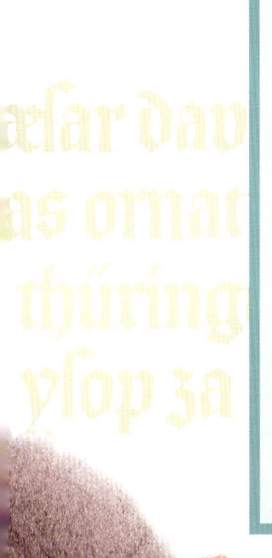

why believe in God?

Part 10

Ow! That hurt!

Why do we have to go through pain, sadness and fear? Another book in this series, Why Believe in Life After Death, *goes into this in more detail. But one reason people give for not believing in God is that such nasty things happen.*

For instance, a brother or sister or best friend gets injured or killed in a road accident. Why did God let it happen?

Or we pray for something not to happen (or to happen), such as getting told off by Mrs Bond at school. But she does.

Why did it happen?

Meningitis is an awful illness which can kill children, especially ones younger than yourself. Now imagine a child, say a five-year-old boy, who is ill in hospital with the disease.

Why do you think things like this happen? Read the ideas and think about them. If you are in a group, discuss them. Decide which reasons are right and which are wrong.

Which did you think most likely? You could say it was the boy's fault, but it's difficult to imagine why a loving God would punish a

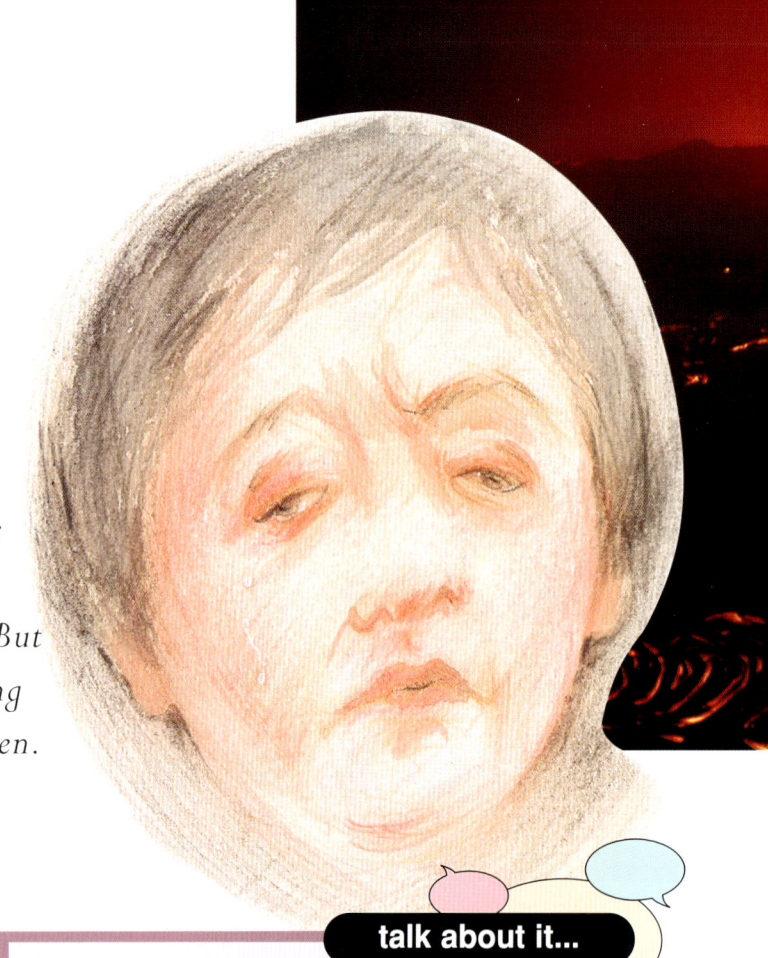

talk about it...

1. The little boy had done something wrong, so God was punishing him.

2. One of the boy's relatives had done something bad, so God was punishing the relative by making them worry about the child.

3. The child caught the disease from somewhere else and there's no reason other than that.

4. Illness is not something God wants to become involved in.

5. Although God has no connection with the illness, we can learn from it.

6. God has a plan to heal suffering.

why believe in God? 23

Above: Natural disasters – such as volcanic eruptions – can cause great hardship. Are they God's responsibility?

Left: Sometimes it can be hard to see why pain is necessary.

little child. Didn't Jesus say, "Let little children come to me!"?

If God is punishing someone else, it seems very hard to use the child in that way.

Surely, it's more likely that the child simply caught the disease, and that's all there is to it. In that case the fourth possible reason seems to follow almost automatically.

As to the fifth, it's quite likely that, even if the worst came to the worst and the little boy died, we'd learn from the experience. It might teach us about caring for others, how to help people to get over bad things or how to cope day after day with something terrible. Whatever, it's very difficult to believe that God would make it happen to the child.

Some people say that God still heals suffering today, just as Jesus did when he was on earth.

You have the same kind of choice. You could choose to give up your seat to an old person on a bus, or help them pick up the groceries they've dropped. Or you could pretend you haven't seen them.

But God sees everything, because he's all knowing. Which must mean that some things happen with the knowledge of God but without God intervening.

Why? One reason could be that it's simply not something God wishes to be involved with. God wants us to become better people, and that means we have to learn from bad things. God doesn't make the bad things (though sometimes we do, with a foolish action). Bad things happen on their own.

And if nothing bad ever happened, how would we know what was good? How could we learn to become better people? We wouldn't have anything with which to compare ourselves or our experiences.

Below: We can learn from pain and sadness, especially if they are shared.

Part 11

That day Auntie tried to eat the lawn

When strange things happen, is it because of us or God? If you had an aunt like mine, you'd know just what I mean. She always seems to be doing something odd – and getting away with it. Once, she rang up a well-known supermarket, dictated a list of groceries to the manager, and said she'd like them delivered the next day.

They were. And the supermarket have delivered her groceries ever since! But I bet if I rang, or if someone you know did, the supermarket would tell us not to be so silly.

Another time, I found her eating a plate of grass clippings, with milk and sugar.

"It's good for you!" she explained. It couldn't have been that good as she never ate any again!

No-one suggests God put these ideas in my Aunt's head. But sometimes, I could imagine God having a good chuckle over her.

There was another side to my aunt. Once, I remember my uncle driving a car along a lane when a woman ran from a house screaming and swearing at us. My uncle

Left: Not many people could get the supermarket to deliver their shopping for free!

why believe in God?

Above: Some people seem to have a special talent for solving other people's problems.

stopped the car and the woman began hitting the car and trying to smash the windows. We didn't know why. I was terrified!

My aunt got out of the car, went to the woman, took a stone calmly from her hand, wrapped her arms round her and gave her a huge, loving hug. My aunt had realised something the rest of us hadn't – that the woman was very distressed by cars.

She took the woman back into her house. While the rest of us sat out in the car wondering what to do, Auntie was inside making her a cup of tea.

Ever after, when we drove past, the woman would come out screaming and swearing as usual until she saw it was us, when she'd open the car door and give my aunt a huge, loving hug before we drove on.

To me, that's one of the ways God works. When something happens, he gives us the chance to do something about it. We don't have to do it, but if we do, we become slightly better people because of it. Not that God puts the chance there, but God – I'm sure – gives us the inner strength to do the thing.

And the physical strength. Once my aunt and I found a very large old man lying on the floor of his kitchen. He'd fallen and couldn't get up. My aunt was half his size, but she picked him up as if he was a bag of sugar.

"Don't just stand there, help me!" she snapped at me. The man seemed incredibly heavy to me, so Auntie said, "Don't bother, I'll manage! God's helping!" She took the pensioner to his armchair and then bustled about making him comfortable and getting a nurse, while I watched on, uselessly.

Again, God doesn't cause these things to happen. And we can ignore them when they do. My aunt doesn't.

I'm sure God had nothing to do with my aunt eating grass clippings. But I am sure that all the things she does for others have made her into a special person. And one of the funny ways she shows how special she is, by doing odd things.

When opportunities happen, and we decide to take them, God helps us. It's something I've seen happen so many times, I'm sure it's true. Are you?

why believe in God?

Part 12

The trial of the century

Left: Most church congregations are older. Are they also wiser?

Have you ever noticed how many old-age pensioners go to church? It's not a new thing — if you could go back in time, you'd see that there were more old people than young in church 20 or 30 years ago, too.

Why do so many older people believe in God? Perhaps it's simply a kind of insurance policy — "I'd better believe, just in case, for when I die." Or have the years made them wiser so that their experiences have left them with far fewer doubts?

for you to try...

This is a trial. You're the judge and the jury. I'm going to present the case. Afterwards, you have the job of deciding. Does God exist? There are twelve reasons, and each one has been explored in a part of this book.

why believe in God? 27

1 Far more people believe in God than don't. Can they all be wrong?

2 The Universe is ordered. Can it all have happened by chance? If it did, where did the original material for the Big Bang come from?

3 It's impossible to think of anything greater than God (said Anselm), so therefore God must exist.

4 People have religious experiences. They couldn't if there was no God.

5 Although we all make mistakes and 'fall down', we're helped to pick ourselves up again. Who by?

6 We're all unique. No other person is exactly the same as us. What – or who – has made us so individual?

7 Not being able to see God doesn't mean God isn't there, any more than hiding a sweet stops it existing.

8 Scientists say we're just animals. Yet there are things about us which make us different from animals, suggesting our creation was not the same as, say, a dog. This means there must be a God involved.

9 Holy books exist and all have parts that are similar to every other. Were they divinely inspired? On the other hand, the differences between them are easily explainable.

10 Why do we have to suffer, if there's a God? Why can't (or won't) God stop it? But suffering makes us learn and grow into better people. And if there weren't bad things, we wouldn't know what was good. So perhaps stopping all suffering isn't part of God's plan – yet.

11 Some people seem to be led by God to do special things. For such people, it seems, there's extra help.

12 Research over many years has shown that, overall, congregations in most – though not all – Christian churches are largely older people. Could this be because older people are wiser?

Now it's your turn to make up your mind. Given all 12 of these reasons, what is your verdict?

Is there a God?

Yes or no?

Or would you rather not have to decide?

Copyright © 1998 Hunt & Thorpe

Text © 1998 Robert Dawson

Illustrations © 1998 Alice Englander

ISBN 1-85608-380-2

Designed by
THE BRIDGEWATER BOOK COMPANY LTD
Designer Andrew Milne

All rights reserved. Except for brief quotation in critical articles or reviews, no part of this book may be reproduced in any manner without prior written permission from the publishers.

Write to:
HUNT & THORPE
Deershot Lodge, Park Lane, Ropley,
nr. Alresford, Hampshire SO24 0BE, UK

Hunt & Thorpe is a name used under licence by Paternoster Publishing, PO Box 300, Kingstown Broadway, Carlisle, CA3 0QS, UK

The right of Robert Dawson to be identified as the author of this work has been asserted in accordance with the Copyright, Designs and Patents Act 1988.

A CIP catalogue record for this book is available from the British Library.

Printed in Singapore